Henry Churchll King

Reconstruction in Theology

Henry Churchill King

Reconstruction in Theology

ISBN/EAN: 9783337175825

Printed in Europe, USA, Canada, Australia, Japan

Cover: Foto ©Lupo / pixelio.de

More available books at **www.hansebooks.com**

Reconstruction in Theology

Henry Churchill King *

1899

RECONSTRUCTION in any living thing is constant, but it may still have its marked stages. To affirm, therefore, that there is need of reconstruction in theology is not at all to overlook the fact that such reconstruction has been constantly going on, that there have been many formulations by individual men more or less satisfactory; but it is simply to say that there is much to indicate that we have reached a point where our great inherited historical statements are quite generally felt to be inadequate, and where conditions, long at work, are so culminating and combining as to give promise of a somewhat marked stage in the development of theology.

Nor does the recognition of the need of reconstruction in Christian theology reflect a feeling of dissatisfaction with the Christian *religion*. On the

---

* "Reconstruction in Theology," *The American Journal of Theology* 3, no. 2 (1899): 295–323. Original version available on the Internet Archive. This version updated June 2, 2017.

contrary, the need of reconstruction is perhaps felt
most strongly by those who have themselves gained
a new sense of the absoluteness of the Christian
religion, and call the old theological statements
in question, because these statements make this
absoluteness so little manifest. Obviously here the
dissatisfaction is not with the Christian religion,
but with our intellectual expression of its meaning.
And it ought not to surprise or trouble us that this
intellectual expression must change from time to
time with other intellectual changes.

There is abundant evidence that the need of reconstruction in theology is widely recognized, but
a single judicious testimony must suffice. In his recent *History of Christian Doctrine*, speaking simply as
a historian, Professor Fisher says:[1] "It is plain to keen
observers that, in the later days, both within and
without what may be called the pale of Calvinism,
there is a certain relaxing of confidence in the previ-
ously accepted solutions of some of the gravest theological problems. This appears among many whose
attachment to the core of the essential truths formu-
lated in the past does not wane, whose substantial
orthodoxy, as well as piety, is not often, if it be at all,
questioned, and who have no sympathy with agnos-
ticism, in the technical sense of the word."

As is implied in this statement of Professor
Fisher's, the reasons for this feeling of need of
reconstruction—to state it summarily—are neither

296

---

[1] p. 551.

a rationalistic spirit in the church, nor the reaction on the church of what is called the anti-religious or anti-Christian spirit of the age. It may be distinctly denied that that spirit is especially characteristic of this age. But the reasons are to be found in a deepening of the Christian spirit itself, and in the *influence of the new intellectual, moral, and spiritual world* in which we live, and upon which this spirit has been working. Just as the acceptance of the principle of the correlation of forces called for a rewriting of physics—a "new physics," or the theory of evolution for the rewriting of biology—a "new biology," so, in the same sense, the acceptance of certain great convictions of our own day calls for a rewriting of theology—a new theology. Not that in any of these cases the great underlying facts have changed, but our conception of them and of their relations has changed. These dominating convictions of our age form a universal permeating atmosphere, which inevitably affects in some way all schools of theology.

What makes this new atmosphere, this new world? What are the convictions increasingly shared by all our generation, whose influence on theology is indubitable and inevitable? It may be worth while, at the risk of rehearsing some familiar facts, to get a clear view of precisely those convictions that make our modern life.

I. THE NEW WORLD

Even a cursory glance discloses many phenomena fairly peculiar to our age, and we are coming to an increasing understanding of the great undercurrents which produce these phenomena. We belong to the modern period, to the nineteenth century, and to the last quarter of the nineteenth century. We inherit all the influences and problems of the past. Historians in all fields recognize the modern period as throughout revolutionary, critical, protestant, but protestant for the sake of reconstruction. This distinguishing characteristic of the new age has been defined as "that enlightenment, destroying in order to reconstruct, which sought to break the dominion of all prejudice, and to undermine every ill-founded belief."[2]

A. IN RELIGION.—The protest began in religion, and was a protest, as Erdmann puts it, on the one hand, against everything in which the church had become secularized, paganized, Judaized; on the other hand, a protest "against everything in which the church had opposed itself to the rational and justifiable interests of the world."[3] Positively the protest meant, as the whole world knows, insistence, in the first place, upon justification by faith and the priesthood of all believers, and, in the second place, the recognition of the rights of property, marriage, and the state. The appeal made in support of these

---

[2] Lotze, *Microcosmus*, Vol. II, p. 286.
[3] *History of Philosophy*, Vol. II, pp. 3, 4.

positions to Scripture and primitive Christianity against the authority of councils and ecclesiastical tradition could end logically only in a defense of entire freedom of conscience and freedom of investigation. This is the only consistent Protestant position.

B. IN THE STATE.—Revolution in the state ends in the practical universal recognition of both absolute natural right and historic legitimate right, as Lotze names them. In this recognition of the double duty of the state—on the one hand, the duty of keeping faith with the past, of preserving some living community with those gone, the conservative tendency, the recognition of historical right; on the other hand, the duty of fidelity to the interests of the present, of revolt against the "dead hand," the radical tendency, the recognition of absolute natural right—in this double recognition lie inclosed all the modern problems of sociology and social evolution.

C. INTELLECTUAL.—In the intellectual sphere the same revolutionary and protestant spirit is to be seen.   298

1. *Modern philosophy* in its rebound from scholastic dogmatism begins with Descartes's "methodical doubt"—the deliberate questioning of everything that could be questioned—and early made its chief investigations in the theory of knowledge, and throughout the period this question has been prominent, if not foremost. That its great subject is man—the whole man—and neither God nor the world, means that it finds its key only in itself, and

not in any external source or authority. Our own century begins with the *Critical Philosophy* of Kant that was intended by its theory of knowledge to make philosophical dogmatism forever impossible. Kant's problems were all problems of mediation and remain essentially the present problems of philosophy, though they are much differently conceived, since the great systems of Fichte, Schleiermacher, Schelling, and Hegel lie between us and Kant. These problems may all be summed up in the problem of bringing into unity the mechanical and ideal views of the world. The last few years have seen the remarkable growth of the newer psychology, the increasing influence of the idea of evolution and the accompanying historical bent of philosophy, and the hardly yet understood complete collapse of materialism as a philosophical theory. The philosophical world is utterly different from that of the Reformation.

2. *In science.*—To the modern period, too, practically belongs the very birth of natural science, in the sense of exact investigation with deliberate experiment and repeated testing. This development of modern science, it has been pointed out, has implied three things: an immensely increased respect for experience, emphasis on the universality of law, and a threefold restriction on the part of science to experience, to a mathematical, not a speculative, development of its data, and to phenomena. That is, modern science distinctly disclaims to be either *a priori*, speculative, or ultimate.

Modern science has besides greatly affected the thought and imagination of men in its immense extension of the world in space and the discernment of its laws through astronomy, and in a similar extension of the world in time and the discernment of its laws through both astronomy and geology.

299

To these influences science has added to the thought of the age a sense of the unity of the world which is fairly overpowering. Extensively, spectrum analysis has been made to testify to uniformity of materials; gravitation and magnetism to uniformity of forces. Intensively, the principle of the conservation of energy is held to prove the unity of all forces, and the theory of evolution aims to include all phenomena under the unity of one method. Practically, scientific inventions have made our earth a unity, in a way not only to affect our imagination, but to change in a marked manner almost all the problems of our time. No man can conceive even superficially the changes involved in the rise of modern science and not feel how impossible it is for men of this generation to occupy precisely the point of view of not more than fifty years ago, even in their theological statements.

3. *In historical criticism.*—In the field of historical criticism our characterization of the intellectual changes which have taken place must be confined to those which bear specially on our theme. "Edwin Hatch," a recent reviewer says, "rejoiced to hear 'the solemn tramp of the science of history marching in our day almost for the first time into the domain of

Christian theology."' The historical sense is itself
almost a product of this century (for it practically
begins with Herder), and it meant real and great
changes, in the first place, in *biblical interpretation*;
since interpretation now seeks to give full weight
to the intellectual, moral, and religious atmosphere
of the time. And to this conviction the immense
increase of the last fifty years in the literature of
the historical criticism of the Bible bears unmis-
takable witness. It was inevitable that the same
historical spirit should recognize differences not
only between Old Testament and New Testament
times, but differences as well within these periods,
and differences also in the point of view of different
classes and individuals in the same period. This
brought into being the whole new science of *biblical
theology*, in which all rejoice, but which, in any strict
construction of it, is less than fifty years old.[4] To
the same historical movement, coupled with literary
300   analysis and carried into the individual books,
belongs the so-called *higher criticism* of the Old
Testament. In its recent really influential form it is
scarcely more than thirty years old, since it virtually
dates from Graf (1866).[5] But far the most important
result of historical criticism for theology has been
what Fairbairn calls "the recovery of the historical
Christ."   It is the unique and greatest service of

---

[4] Cf. OEHLER, *Theology of the Old Testament*, pp. 32 ff.
[5] Cf. BRIGGS, *The Higher Criticism of the Hexateuch*, pp. 90 ff.
See also PFLEIDERER, *The Development of Theology*, pp. 258 ff.

Principal Fairbairn's epoch-making book on The Place of Christ in Modern Theology that it makes so clear the place that Christ occupies in the thought of our generation. "Our day," he says, "has also been marked by a return to the sources of a quite specific character—it has been more distinctly than any other a return to the historical Christ . . . .—to him as the person who created alike the evangelists and the apostles, by whom he is described and interpreted."[6]

Let one bring together now, for a moment, in thought the intellectual changes in philosophy, in science, and in historical criticism of the last seventy years, and he must agree with John Fiske that "in their mental habits, in their methods of inquiry, and in the data at their command, the men of the present day who have fully kept pace with the scientific movement are separated from the men whose education ended in 1830 by an immeasurably wider gulf than has ever before divided one progressive generation of men from their predecessors."[7] If the man of today, therefore, is really alive to the movements of his own time, it is simply impossible that he should use most naturally and easily the language of the older generation in expressing his deepest convictions on any theme.

D. MORAL AND SPIRITUAL.—Side by side with the revolution in religion, in the state, and in the

---

[6] *The Place of Christ in Modern Theology*, p. 187.

[7] *The Idea of God*, p. 56.

intellectual sphere, and influenced by these, there have taken place in the modern period similar changes in the general moral and spiritual convictions. Is it possible to state with some clearness and precision, and yet with the utmost brevity and without argument, the greatest of these fundamental moral and spiritual convictions of our day?—(1) From modern humanism, the special influence, most of all of Christianity, but also of political and social evolution, of philosophy, and the newer psychology, has come a greatly heightened sense of the *value and sacredness of the individual person* in his entirety. Sensitiveness as to the personal throughout is stronger, as it ought to be, than in any preceding period, and under it may be brought almost every other moral characteristic of our age.—(2) From the whole spirit of the modern period, but especially from Protestantism, and the influence of philosophy and of science, has come, we may hope, finally full recognition of *freedom of conscience* and *freedom of investigation*. These principles are distinctly moral, though applied in the intellectual sphere.—(3) The influence of natural science, moreover, has been effective in bringing into clear consciousness Christianity's latent *recognition of law, conditions, and time* in the moral and spiritual life, as truly as in any other sphere.—(4) The idealistic trend in philosophy, so strongly asserted by Paulsen and evidenced by the collapse of materialism, and the teleological view of evolution, added to the constant pressure of the Christian spirit, have made two closely connected convictions increasingly dominant: that, in the order of the universe, *the mechanical is means only*, and that the *unity of the ethical life is found in love*. Even where not distinctly affirmed, but perhaps even questioned, it is believed that these two convictions are really present as fundamental assumptions in the reasoning of our time.—(5) Out of Protestantism in its original criticism of Catholicism, out of philosophy in its emphasis on man as *both* microcosmus and microtheos, and out of science with its implied trend toward the doctrine of divine immanence, has grown the *denial of the separation of the sacred and the secular*.—(6) From the growing sense of the worth of personality, helped particularly by the immensely deepened knowledge of "the other half," and the great influence of the analogy of the organism in the history of thought, has developed the *social conscience* of our time—the definite avowal that we are all members one of another.—(7) The new psychology, too, the latest conspicuous intellectual movement of our day, has not only confirmed the other tendencies already named, but has also added one distinctive contribution of rapidly growing influence—*the central importance of action*. Body and mind, we are made for action. Nor is this a rebound to a new extreme. The natural terminus of all experiences, bodily and mental, is action. For the very sake, therefore, of thought and feeling, one must act. The emphasis on action is, indeed, a protest against mere intellectualism or romanticism, but it is at the same time an insistence on the unity

302

of man, and on the *whole* man.—(8) And historical criticism has not only strengthened the emphasis on the historical, the concrete, and personal, but has brought into the very foreground the greatest of all spiritual influences, *the practical Lordship of Christ.* "This is not," it has been well said, "an individual or incidental thing, but represents the tide and passion of the time; is, as it were, the sum and essence of the living historical, philosophical, and religious spirit."[8]

These, then, we may believe, if we have succeeded in correctly discerning the trend of the modern age, are the fundamental moral and spiritual convictions of our time: reverence for personality, freedom of conscience, and freedom of investigation; law in the spiritual world, yet the subordination of the mechanical, and the unity of the ethical life in love; no separation of the sacred and secular; the social conscience, the central importance of action, the recognition of Christ as the supreme person.

They are not wholly new—of course not, and they have not grown up in a night, as their sources plainly show; but their present emphasis is relatively new, and on the farther side of these convictions lies, not our world, but another. And an age in whose life and thought they are working like yeast simply cannot express itself adequately in the terms of statements made when these convictions were

---

[8] FAIRBAIRN, op. cit, p. 188.

not so felt, and it would be no real service to the church if it could, for it belongs to the very nature of spiritual truth that each age must be its own interpreter in spiritual things.

II. THE INEVITABLE INFLUENCE OF THIS NEW WORLD ON THEOLOGY

Now, it is this new world in which we think and live that is the one great source of our dissatisfaction with the older statements in theology. These ruling ideas of our time are constantly at work. We all accept them more or less fully in themselves, and they are certain to prevail increasingly, and their ultimate influence in theology is simply inevitable, and ought to be. What, now, do they mean for theology?

In attempting to indicate some of the ways in which it seems that the atmosphere of our time (so far as it is right) is certain to affect theological statements, one can only bear honest testimony as to the direction in which progress seems to lie for our own generation. In a time of transition like the present it is impossible for any man to speak with frankness and definiteness on theological themes and command the assent of all, or perhaps the full assent of any. But truth comes, not through the silence of all, but by each declaring honestly and earnestly his best. Honest, thoughtful testimony, charitably and reverently borne, is the greatest need of the immediate present, if we are ever to come to that better intellectual expression of Christianity for which all wait.

A. MAINLY INTELLECTUAL INFLUENCES.—1. In the first place, the Protestant principle of *freedom of investigation* means the full recognition of the legitimacy, value, and authority of literary, historical, and scientific investigation in its own sphere—that of the tracing of causal connections. It means that theology refuses to settle *a priori* how God *must* have acted in any case in nature or in revelation, but turns over to humble, patient, scientific inquiry to determine how he *did* and *does* act. All questions, thus, of natural or mechanical *process* by which things came to be what they now are are unreservedly committed to scientific investigation. This means, *e.g.*, that all questions as to the conditions of the appearance of life, of man, of conscience, and all questions of the method of God's historical self-revelation, all questions of the authorship, age, and unity of the Scriptures, are to be freely and fearlessly investigated in a strictly scientific way. Scientific investigation can only make more clear to us exactly how God did proceed. And this, if we are really in earnest in our desire to understand God, we ought to be glad to know. If tomorrow men were able to trace in the laboratory the precise steps by which the living arises from the non-living, or if in some historical seminar the exact source and composition of Isaiah could be demonstratively made out, no ideal or religious interest would be in any manner affected, except that we should simply understand a little more fully the method God took in a case in which the mode of his action is to us now quite obscure. Our only anxiety can be that the investigators be really competent, and particularly in the investigation of moral and religious problems competence requires personal experience in the sphere investigated. It is, therefore, the poorest possible policy for the church to warn off its own scholars from these investigations. Moreover, the only answer to erroneous criticism is better criticism, not the forbidding of criticism. And the latter, we may be sure, is no service to the church, by whomsoever advocated. As Julius Müller long ago said: "Wounds which have been inflicted on humanity by knowledge can be healed only by knowledge." This is the one sure road to peace. Of these scientific investigations theology simply takes the results. It is itself strictly an interpretative science, and it reserves to itself the right to interpret the results of scientific inquiry. It leaves absolutely to science the tracing of the causal connections; it claims for itself the ideal interpretation. The process belongs to science, the meaning to theology.

2. *Its relation to natural science.*—Of the purely intellectual influences on theology in our day that of natural science is particularly strong. We cannot, therefore, avoid, in the second place, the question of the relation of natural science to theology. What does the influence of natural science mean for theology?

It is well to notice at the very start that it is easy to overestimate the importance of this relation and the extent of this influence; and both are often overestimated, I believe, today. Professor James 305 puts the matter in his usual vigorous fashion, when he says: "The aspiration to be scientific is such an idol of the tribe to the present generation, is so sucked in with his mother's milk by every one of us, that we find it hard to conceive of a creature who should not feel it, and harder still to treat it freely as the altogether peculiar and one-sided subjective interest which it is."[9] Nevertheless, the immense progress and rightful influence of natural science in our own generation force upon theology (in its wider sense) the problem of the mediation of the mechanical and ideal views of the world. Of the ultimate solution of the problem Christian theology can have no doubt, for it is involved in the central faith in a *God of love.* And, meanwhile, it addresses itself without misgivings to the adjustment of its relation to natural science.

(1) It accepts, in the first place, *science's own restrictions of itself* to experience, to the tracing of purely causal connections, and to phenomena. This restriction necessarily excludes all questions of ultimate origin and destiny. The scientific question is one of *process* merely. And, as no one thinks of seeing God at work like a man in the changes of nature, the process would seem the same to the observer, whether he thought it purely mechanical or wholly due to God.

(2) Secondly, it accepts unreservedly science's main contention of the *universality of law,* that mechanism is absolutely universal in extent, though

---

[9] *Psychology*, Vol. II, p. 640.

it requires that the principle shall be exactly defined.
It asks, *i. e.*, that it shall be noted that the principle is
universality of law, not, as much talk would seem to
imply, *uniformity* of law. There has been an amazing
haziness concerning this simple point. The true
scientific contention is, not that laws are always and
everywhere the same, but that there is always law.
With this guarding of the principle theology may
well not only accept, but itself vigorously affirm on
ideal grounds, the universality of law. Religion has
as great an interest as science in asserting a sphere
of law. For a sphere of law is necessary in order to
any growth in *knowledge* through experience, since,
if there were no law, nothing learned today would   306
be of any value tomorrow. Nor could there be any
growth in *power* without law, for all our power of
accomplishment depends wholly on knowledge of
the laws of the forces with which we deal. Growth
in *character*, moreover, is similarly conditioned.
A sphere of law, therefore, is the only possible
sphere for a progressive being, and it is precisely
his progressiveness—his capacity of indefinite
growth—that mainly distinguishes man intellectually from the lower animals; and with man all ideal
interests come in. It is to be further noticed that a
sphere of law is necessary to give any significance to
freedom itself, the condition of character; for choices
look to ends, and there can be no accomplishment
of an end without law. For another reason, too,
religion can brook no lawless world; for to allow
such a world would make God play fast and loose

with his creatures. In order to faith in the fidelity and trustworthiness of God himself, therefore, there must be law. In its own distinct sphere of the moral and spiritual life, moreover, theology distinctly welcomes the idea of law. Drummond, more than any other man, has brought this home to the religious consciousness of our generation, and it is his greatest contribution—*not* that there is the *same* law for the natural and spiritual world (as he at first affirmed), but that there *is* law; that there are definite conditions to be fulfilled for any spiritual attainment, that these conditions may be known, and that when fulfilled you may count on the results. Theology has much to gain in clearness and precision of statement, and in power of appeal, in development of this line of thought.

The whole ideal contention and the interest of theology, therefore, is not at all against law, against mechanism; it must rather, with science, insist upon law; it *is* that mechanism is means only, and means must not be mistaken for ends nor dominate ends. Exactly here lies the religious interest in *miracle*. The insistence on miracle for the religious man means the insistence on a living God, and the insistence that, though mechanism is absolutely universal in extent, nevertheless, as Lotze says, "it is completely subordinate in significance." We are not to make a god of mechanism, it declares, nor put mechanism above God. The universality of law, therefore, is to theology only the perfect consistency in the modes of activity of God in carrying out his immutable purpose of love. Hence, God will always act according to law—that is, in perfect consistency with his unchanging purpose of love; but his action may not always be formulable under any of the laws of nature known to us. "*All's* love, yet *all's* law."

(3) In the third place, in the relation of theology to natural science, theology accepts from natural science the *theory of evolution* as a general statement of the method of God's working, and renews in consequence its own older emphasis upon the immanence of God.

Here, too, it wishes only that there should be real precision of thought as to what the evolution theory is. It has a suspicion that, as in many another case, difficulty comes only because the principle is not carried completely through. The trouble in evolution is that we are only *half* evolutionists. Theology is interested only to insist that evolution means real evolution—a succession of stages with new phenomena and new laws (and this the law of cyclical movement itself asserts), and that it *does not stop with the animal series*, but includes the human stage. It insists, therefore, that evolution does not mean the putting of everything on a dead level, especially not a degrading of everything to the lowest level, but that when the new appears it is really *new*—it has not appeared before. It may be assumed, as in the development of the individual, that the process is ever so gradual, and that the power is there ready to appear when the conditions for its appearance are completed; but when the new power appears—life, self-

consciousness, moral responsibility, or what not—it
is really new. It had not appeared before. Courtney[10]
maintained the whole ideal contention more fully,
perhaps, than he knew, when he wrote fifteen years
ago: "I *was* an anthropoid ape once, a mollusc, an as-
cidian, a bit of protoplasm; but, whether by chance
or providence, I am not now. When I was an ape, I
thought as an ape, I acted as an ape, I lived as an ape;
but when I became a man, I put away apish things.
Man's moral nature is what it is, not what it was."

If, then, that conception of evolution is maintained which its own definition and laws require,
theology finds no religious or ideal consideration
that need hinder it in accepting the most absolute
and radical form of the evolution theory without
any thought of intervention at any point in the
process. It feels no interest in insisting upon certain
unbridged gaps in the series as essential at all to
a religious view of the world. The most absolute
evolution theory, so long as it is scientific at all, can
be only a description of the process by which God
has worked, of the method which he has employed.
Theology is perfectly ready to accept the facts,
whatever they may be. As it has been well said:
"Whichever way of creation God may have chosen,
in none can the dependence of the universe on him
become slacker, in none be drawn closer."[11]

And more than this is true. Not only is the reli-

---

[10] *Studies in Philosophy*, chap. vi.
[11] Lotze, *op. cit.*, Vol. I, p. 374.

gious interest here not opposed to the scientific; in one important particular it is identical with it. For its own sake, theology can remain satisfied no longer with the old, inconsistent view of a virtual independence of the world in the larger part of it, and of direct dependence on God at certain points only, where we cannot yet trace the process of God's working. It is quite unwilling to say God is only where we cannot understand him. It is quite unwilling to admit that increasing knowledge of God's working is progressive elimination of God from the universe. It is quite unwilling to take its stand on gaps or base its arguments for God on ignorance. It believes in God—in a God upon whom the whole universe, in every least atom of it, and in every humblest spirit of it, is absolutely dependent. Of that dependence it is certain, and no study of the *method* of it can make it less certain.

Theology rejoices, then, in the larger view evolution seems to give of the method, plan, and aim of God in the universe; in the great extension and strengthening of the design argument; in the harmony it brings into the divine methods, and in the enlarged conception of God in his immanence in the world.

309

Outside of these general gains which the evolution theory seems to bring, and in which most would probably agree, exactly what does the detailed application of evolution to theological and ethical problems mean? Is there not much confusion of thought here that seems often to end only in juggling with

phrases, both on the side of the mechanical philoso-
pher and on the side of the religious apologist?

If the *entire* evolution series, including man, with
his moral and spiritual nature, is meant, then the
later stages will be recognized, according to the law
of cyclical movement, as higher, and as having their
own peculiar phenomena and laws, and interpreted
accordingly, but with due regard to the lower stages.

If the *purely animal organic evolution* is meant,
then the analogy is taken wholly from the realm
below man; and, however suggestive, must obviously, on the principle of evolution itself, prove
inadequate for an interpretation of the intellectual,
moral, and spiritual life of man, and must finally
break down, as it does even in the hands of so skilful
and sympathetic an interpreter as Drummond. The
analogy of organic evolution is only the farthest
possible extension of the very fruitful analogy of the
organism that has been so influential in the history
of thought from Paul to Shaftesbury and Kant, and
down to modern ethics and sociology. It is the most
adequate analogy that nature furnishes us, and it
is *useful* to apply it as fully as possible in order to
discern the essential harmony of the laws in all the
stages, and to see that the natural world is from
the same hand as the moral; but, after all is said,
it is still only an analogy from nature, and quite
inadequate to set forth all the life of the spirit in
itself and its personal relations. We are spirits, not
organisms, and society is a society of persons, not
an organism. The theory of the evolution of the

animal series, fully accepted, therefore, in its most radical form, is still no universal solvent of ethical and theological questions where personal relations replace organic. It is a perversion of the evolution theory in its real entirety to attempt to bring all the higher stages under the laws of the lower. Yet this is what the application of evolution to theology and ethics seems to mean to many. The inadequacy of 310 the method is seen from the way in which many of the most serious difficulties have to be solved by bringing in considerations entirely apart from evolution. Although, therefore, the writer shares with the enthusiastic advocates of evolution in theology the freest acceptance of evolution in its fullest form, he does not have their confidence in its wonder-working power in theology. It is true that the attempt to state the entire ethical or sociological or theological problem in biological terms—in terms of life—of organic evolution, is very fascinating and sounds very scientific; but in truth its success is its failure, for it can succeed only by forgetting the essential nature of that with which it is dealing—spirit, not physical life. Guardedly used, the analogy is helpful, but adequate it never is. On the human stage of evolution we have reached persons and personal relations, and the laws are those of personal relations. God will deal with us on this stage in accordance with the principle of evolution, if he deals with us as persons and enters into personal relations with us. And this Christianity has always believed. The application of evolution here will simply mean, therefore, that in these personal relations with men God's self-revelation at every stage will be adapted to men's capacities to receive, and will progress as rapidly as possible; that the complete revelation in Christ comes as soon as there are men who can use it with value and preserve it for a progressive evaluation by those who follow. We have no call to show that in these personal relations of men with men, or of God with men, all that occurs can be brought under the laws that hold on the lower stages. It is vain, therefore, to look for revolutionary results in the statement of individual theological doctrines from the theory of evolution in its narrower scope. Helpful analogies and suggestive points of view we shall have, but scarcely more. But the legitimate application of evolution in its entirety is a thing to be welcomed, not feared. All God's ways are harmonious.

3. *As necessarily affected by historical criticism.*—Of the mainly intellectual influences on theology, the most important must be that of historical criticism. Christianity is preeminently a historical religion, and such persistent and painstaking historical researches as those of the last sixty years must help us to more accurate and illuminating statements. Theology can be certain that the assured results of patient investigation (it is quite too early to dogmatize as to details in higher criticism, if we can ever do so), because they will show us more perfectly the method that God actually did take in his revelation of himself to men, will bring, not disaster, but great enrichment to

311

theology. His ways are higher than our ways, and his thoughts than our thoughts. Some of the adjustments required will in the time of transition no doubt seem difficult and even threatening; but it is certain that, so far as we are able actually to find God's way—and this is the sole final result of historical criticism—it will be *better* than our way. And the time is not far distant, we may believe, when we shall enumerate the blessings of critical investigation, including the higher criticism. We shall rejoice in the better understanding of God involved in the more vivid setting forth of his persistent, patient, loving adaptation to men; we shall, indeed, have lost a uniform authoritative lawbook, but we shall have gained instead a living revelation of a living God in living men, rich and throbbing as life itself; we shall be grateful that the phenomena of the Bible disclosed by patient study *compelled* us to a restatement of the doctrine of inspiration that eliminated from it the mechanical, and brought it into full accord with the working of God in our own hearts as promised by Christ—never God alone, and never man alone, but always God and man, in a personal cooperation that means character and love. We shall come to see with some surprise that a view of inspiration as really moral and spiritual, with its natural implications, has practically removed all our own difficulties concerning the Bible and disposed of the main attacks upon it, at the same time.

Positively for theology these implications of the changed view of inspiration, which the results of his-

torical criticism require, include, in the first place, a
much fuller recognition of the principle of *progress
in revelation*, that this involves inevitably the relative
imperfection of the earlier stages and makes Christ
the absolute standard in the Bible as well as out of
it. Theology never had any need to affirm any other
principle than this, but it has certainly not yet fully
adjusted itself to this fact.

Further, this study of the Bible itself has brought
out into striking light its one great *purpose* in absolute
agreement with Paul's own clear statement[12]—that it
is neither science nor history, but solely and simply
a record of the historical self-revelation of God to a
single people and so to all men. This means that,
even in books called historical, its writers are not interested in strict scientific history at all, any more
than in some other books they are interested in pure
natural science. Nature and history both concerned
them only as revelations of God. A complete account
of either lies quite outside their task. They select
only those features that can be turned to religious account. They make no attempt to trace all the causal
connections; they *do* seek to show what both nature
and, especially, history *mean* for religion—how God
reveals himself in them. Because they concentrated
themselves upon this one task, they are the world's
teachers in neither science, nor history, nor law, nor
art, nor philosophy—but we all sit at their feet in
religion. Even the historical writers, especially in

[12] 2 Tim. 2:16-17.

312 (margin)

the Old Testament, are, therefore, properly prophets, preaching from historical texts, and the Jews rightly called them so.

In the third place, this more careful biblical study is making clear, what a really spiritual view of inspiration would lead us to expect, that, with all its wonderful unity of development, there is no mechanical unity in the Bible or even the New Testament, but that the different writers show *individual reflections* of a religious experience more or less common to them. In the New Testament this gives individual reflections of Christ. It is in this very way that we are able to approach any adequate conception of the real significance of Christ, and of that larger unity which comes from him and not from the single expression of even his greatest disciple. No one view, no single expression, can suffice. The work of Christ is deeper and broader than any single statement of it, even in Scripture. The recognition of this fact has promise, not only of a reasonable freedom for theology, but of large growth as well, and of a better appreciation of the richness of the New Testament testimony itself.

313

B. MORAL AND SPIRITUAL INFLUENCES.—When we turn from the mainly intellectual influences on theology to those distinctly moral and spiritual, we may perhaps group them all under the two heads of the deepening sense of the value and sacredness of the person, and the growing recognition of Christ as the supreme person.

I . *The inevitable influence on theology of the sense of the value and sacredness of personality.*—The greatest outcome of an advancing civilization is the deepening sense of the value of the individual person. This is the very flower and test of civilization. If it be true, as was said, that the sensitiveness as to the personal throughout is stronger in our age than in any preceding, this is certain in time to influence theology profoundly. It affects at once our view of inspiration and our whole doctrine of the spirit in its hidden working, and throws light on the providence of God, on the meaning of prayer, and on the obscurity of spiritual truth; as well as affects the tone of the presentation of every doctrine.

(1) Out of it grows at once the obligation of love, and of a love that not only includes all persons, but that is such a love as to include all virtues. It means, therefore, a true humanism, but no sentimentalism, for it looks only to the complete character. This *unity of the ethical life in love* is the first clear step in an ultimate philosophy; it is the most important inheritance left us by Edwards; it is soundly biblical; and it is constantly gaining ground. But it is still fully recognized by few in theology. The old dualism of justice and love, or holiness and love, still works confusion in both ethics and theology. It is still too largely felt that there is division in God, that nature, law, and grace root in different purposes, instead of all working to the same end. Even those who have meant wholly to accept the all-embracing character of love have seldom carried it fearlessly out for God and for man at all times and in all conditions. But to carry entirely through this principle of the unity of the eth-

ical life in love is the only logical consequence of the present sense of the value of the person. "Not that   314 we love God, but that he loved us." "Every one that loveth is begotten of God and knoweth God."

And it is the very sense of the sacredness and value of the person which has brought about the "reduction of the area of Calvinism" of which Fisher speaks. It is simply impossible to hold to arbitrary decrees in the old sense in the face of this conviction. The reaction, also, by elaborate argument and labored exegesis against the universal fatherhood of God, that all men as men are the children of God, is for a like reason simply hopeless. The conviction of the fatherhood of God has grown directly out of the representation of God by Christ, and its connection with the root cannot be severed by ever so elaborate an argument.

(2) The deepening sense of the worth of the person means, in the second place, the *recognition of the whole man*. The whole man is expressed only in personal relations. Theology accepts heartily psychology's new assertion of the unity of man, and seeks to take account of the entire spirit. It believes with modern philosophy that man is the key to all problems, but only the whole man. If I do not mistake the drift of modern thinking, it is in essential agreement with Lotze's main contention, "that the nature of things does not consist in thoughts, and that thinking is not able to grasp it; yet perhaps the whole mind experiences in other forms of its action and passion the essential meaning of all

being and action, thought subsequently serving it as an instrument, by which that which is thus experienced is brought into the connection which its nature requires, and is experienced in more intensity as the mind is master of this connection.'[13] This is no underrating of the intellectual, but an insistence that man is more than intellect, and, therefore, that an adequate philosophy, no less than an adequate theology, must take account of all the data—emotional and volitional as well as intellectual; aesthetic, ethical, and religious as well as mechanical. It is a revolt against a misnamed rationalism that knows only intellect, in favor of a genuine rationalism that knows the whole man. It believes, therefore, with Armstrong's putting of Seth's position, that "the language of morality or religion, the language which speaks of God in terms of our own highest experience, is really *truer* than purely metaphysical language concerning God *can be*. 'Religion and higher poetry . . . . carry us nearer to the meaning of the world than the formulæ of an abstract metaphysics."'

(3) In the third place, this emphasis on the personal means for theology *the exclusion of the mechanical* (as contrasted with the spiritual) every-where. It is noticeable that all agree essentially in this aim of excluding the mechanical, though they do not agree as to what is mechanical. It is this spirit that makes it so certain that the attempt to press the

---

[13] *Op. cit.*, Vol. II, pp. 359, 360.

analogy of the lower evolution is wrong. It is this that leads strong conservatives like Frank, liberals like Pfleiderer, and Ritschlians like Herrmann, all alike, to emphasize the importance of the inner spiritual evidence to Christianity. This movement logically requires of theology that it do not stop until it interpret all its strictly theological problems in terms of personal relation. The relations are nowhere more intensely personal. Theology will yet put more meaning than it ever has put into Christ's declaration: "This is life eternal, that they should *know thee* the only true God, and him whom thou didst send, even Jesus Christ." Deepening acquaintance with God is the one all-embracing problem of the Christian life; every step of it is a personal relation; and its laws are the laws of friendship. This steady and certain movement away from the mechanical to the personal is the inner ground of dissatisfaction with all natural, legal, and governmental analogies, applied, *e.g.*, to the doctrine of the atonement. The deep significance of Dr. Trumbull's exhaustive survey in his remarkable books on *The Blood Covenant* and *The Threshold Covenant* is that he traces back so clearly analogies that have been otherwise interpreted to the closest personal relations. And yet the more or less mechanical analogies will pass away as only subordinately helpful, not because they are attacked from without, but because, in the deepening sense of the intensely personal nature of the relations involved, the basis of their appeal will have broken down within. They will be set aside, not because they make too much of the work of Christ in his life or death, but because they make too little of it; because they leave our relation to him still too external and mechanical, and fail to bring it home to us as a moral reality. The more personal view believes that more truly and really than any other it can say: "He was wounded for our transgressions; he was bruised for our iniquities; the chastisement of our peace was upon him; and with his stripes we are healed."

This interpretation of all strictly theological problems in terms of personal relations will bring great gain to theology in both simplicity and unity; it will make theology *seem* to many less scientific, because it will have dropped much technical language which has no longer any proper application; but it will have *deepened* in the same proportion the perception of the real spiritual problems, and will lean more on psychology and ethics, and less on metaphysics and jurisprudence.

(4) The denial of the separation between sacred and secular things, which also grows out of the sense of the sacredness of personality, looks to the inevitable *rejection of all sacramentalism* as necessarily mechanical. It knows no sacred things, but only sacred persons. The sacredness of things and places and times is wholly borrowed from persons. And between things no line is to be drawn of sacred and secular. "All things are yours," and all are means only, but all may be made means. There is to be

war on the worldly spirit, but not on the world.
We are to be in the world, though not of the world.
It is by no means unimportant to a theology that
intends to keep itself free from mere mechanism
and superstition to see clearly two sides of the truth:
that the most holy things are so only because they
minister to the spirit of a living person, and that *all*
things are to be so used as to give this ministration.
If one chooses to say so, this is to make all things
sacramental; but this is the death of the older
sacramentalism which lives on the assertion of the
sole virtue of certain things. Just now the doctrine
of the incarnation is being widely used to put new
life into sacramentalism; but it is only the sound
of the word, not its true meaning, which gives the   317
view any support. The revelation of God in Christ is
beyond all else personal, and only personal; it is no
mere toying with the flesh of humanity. The church
is no institution, but, as Fairbairn says, "the church
is the *people* of God; wherever they are he is, and the
church through him in them."[14]

(5) The *intense quickening of the social conscience*,
too, which also is born of the sense of the worth
of the person, cannot help deepening our insight
into another side of biblical and Christian teaching.
This is for theology simply the clear recognition of
the large place given to the kingdom of God in the
teaching of Christ. The astonishment is that, even
apart from the explicit teaching as to the kingdom,

---

[14] *Op. cit.*, p. 530.

with Christ's statement of the great commandment
before men, any other view could have been held.
Flight from the world, and flight from human
relations, were no legitimate growth from the spirit
of Christ. In any case it would seem that we can
never again forget that "we are members one of
another." And few principles have so many vital
applications in theology. As certain as that the great
commandment is love and that the great means to
character is association, so certain is it that we are
necessary one to another. As certain as that each has
his own individual outlook on the divine, so certain
is it that we need to share each other's visions. The
principle sheds its light on the problem of evil, and
on the meaning of intercessory prayer, and on many
another dark place in our thinking. Only through
it is the full greatness of the human spirit seen, and
the largeness of the life open to it, for it implies the
divine friendship as well. All this is true, and much
more. But we must not make here another false
application of the analogy of the organism. To press,
as many are now doing, the analogy of the organism
is really to repudiate that out of which the whole
development of the social conscience has come—the
sense of the value of the individual person.

(6) Every one of these considerations drawn
from emphasis on the personal implies an *increasing
emphasis on the ethical* that affects theology at every
318   point. The very definition of religion is changed.
The separation of the ethical and religious is becom-
ing impossible. The reality of the moral life of man

seems to us now one of the main foundations of a religious view. And we can conceive no salvation that does not include character. We believe that the ethical is *always* involved in every genuine religious experience. As Herrmann puts it: "Neither in what is opposed to duty, nor in what is indifferent to it, can we meet with God, or do we desire to do so."[15] We are compelled, therefore, to a reinterpretation of the Reformation formula. We see with Paul in faith a real personal relation, but one that is the germ of *real* righteousness. To deny all worth to faith, any activity on the part of man, is simply to deny that that has taken place which it is the whole aim of redemption to bring about—the voluntary choosing to be a child of God, of like character with him. A thoroughly ethical conception of salvation affects theological statements in unlooked-for ways, and to an extent impossible even to indicate. It is no denial of a real forgiveness of sins, but it makes sin not less but more serious. On the other hand, it puts an absolute bar to the older Calvinism of salvation by divine decree, supposing that that made conceivable the idea of character at all. The atonement, too, can get its full meaning only as it is conceived as ethical *throughout*.

(7) And if theology accepts the guidance, not only of ethics, but also of psychology, with what Paulsen calls its "voluntaristic trend," it must be *practical*. Certainly in religion—giving principles

---

[15] *Communion with God*, p. 106.

for life, a method of living—if anywhere, judgment
by consequences ought to apply. Moreover, all
doctrine is originally only the thought expression
of experience or its supposed implications, and has,
therefore, a solely practical source. And all doctrine
must have meaning for life. It must be seen to bear
on life; something must follow from it for attitude
and conduct. This is the very ground of distinction
between other truth and moral and spiritual truth.
The latter is always an appeal to character. If it is
not so, we may be very sure it is not correctly stated.
The New England theologians, therefore, rightly
sought a theology that could be *preached.* So far as
319   theology is a science of practical religion, the test
is genuine and needed, but it would cut severely
much that goes under the name of theology.

   2. *The influence on theology of the recognition of
Christ as the supreme person.*—All these deeper moral
convictions of our time which we have been consid-
ering lead naturally to the recognition of Christ as
the supreme person, and therefore the supreme fact
of history, and the supreme revelation of God, and
this recognition in turn strengthens all the other convictions. This growing convergence of the thought
of the world toward Christ is far the greatest fact of
our time. At the end of every path there looms up
before us this one great towering figure. The simple
truth is that we stand face to face with the historical
Christ, as it has been said, "in a sense and to a
degree unknown to the church since the apostolic
age." It is a most significant fact that every single

great life of Christ since the gospels is the product
of but little more than the last sixty years. Every
ray of light, historical, critical, philosophic, ethical,
religious, has been concentrated upon him. No such
study was ever given to any theme. It would be
criminal thoughtlessness that could make that fact
without effect in theology. Better to know Christ is
certainly to be able to speak more adequately about
him. And it would be our shame, not the glory of
the Fathers, if in spite of the deepening knowledge
of Christ, we were content to speak precisely as they
spoke. We would much better try to speak as we
believe they would speak now. The very movement
itself makes it certain, however, that this is not to
make Christ less, but more.

(1) The recovery of the historical Christ, this
growing recognition of his supremacy, means for
theology, then, in the first place, that it accepts Christ
in truth as the *supreme* revelation of God, its one
great source of the knowledge of God's character
and purpose. With this fact it is in dead earnest.
It does not deny that there are other sources, but
it holds them to be distinctly subordinate. Christ
and only Christ is adequate to give the Christian
conception of God. It welcomes gladly all other
light, and it knows that the mind must do its best
to bring into unity all its possessions, but natural   320
theology is for it supplementary rather than basic,
subordinate to, not coordinate with, Christ. It
seeks with all earnestness approximation to *Christ's*
theology. It erects no altar to an unknown God; it

takes refuge in neither scholasticism nor mysticism. It knows one God, the God revealed in Christ, and it accepts with confidence the affirmation of Christ: "He that hath seen me hath seen the Father; how sayest thou, show us the Father?"

The cry "Back to Christ" means for theology that Christ is really supreme, in the Bible and out of it. And it believes that any reaction against the cry so interpreted is doomed to failure. Theology must recognize the indispensable value of the apostolic testimony to Christ, but it must reserve the right (and it is vain to deny it) by legitimate historical criticism to appeal from the reflection of Christ to the Christ reflected. That Christ is Lord ought to be no divisive cry for any disciple of Christ.

(2) And of the character of the God who reveals himself in Christ theology can have no doubt. It sees *God in Christ*; it knows and seeks no better name for him than Christ's own constantly repeated name, Father. And when it seeks to interpret that name by Christ's own spirit in life and death, it seems for the first time really to know what love and what sin are. God is no longer onlooker, nor even sovereign merely; but Father, holy and loving, who because he hates sin and knows its awfulness, and yet loves with surpassing love his child, suffers in the sin of his child. It is no sentimentalism. The more the Father loves the child, the more he hates the sin of the child, and must use every means to put the sin away. On the other hand, the revelation of the Father alone brings his sin adequately to the man himself. It puts

his sin in the light of the suffering love of God, of what it costs the Father's heart, and brings home so the shame of it and the guilt of it as no punishment could possibly do. Christ's conception of God as Father, as Fairbairn justly says, must be taken as the really ruling conception, determining all else in theology.

(3) Historical criticism has brought us also into the very presence of the *man* Jesus, and has renewed for us, therefore, the gospel's own emphasis on the humanity of Christ, almost forgotten by the church in spite of both gospels and creeds. But it is most significant that it is directly through this study of the humanity of Jesus that his lordship and divinity have become so plain. It is no Unitarian drift which the age has disclosed, and yet it accepts the emphasis on Christ's humanity. The religious need of the humanity of Christ is very great, for otherwise his whole life is unreal, and has no true relation to our life, and he could give to us no perfect revelation of the perfect filial relation to God. But more than this is true. It is supremely in the *character* of Christ that God stands fully revealed, and this character must be real—the real character of the man Jesus. His true humanity is, therefore, essential to the revelation of his divinity. The two stand in closest relation. Not God *and* man, but God revealed because true man.

(4) But there is one inference widely drawn from this newly awakened belief in the divinity of Christ, against which, it seems to the writer, earnest and honest protest should be made. The evangelical

321

church knows well, with van Dyke,[16] that "the unveiling of the Father in Christ was and continued to be, and still is, the palladium of Christianity;" and no age has had a more thorough and intelligent conviction of the lordship and divinity of Christ than ours. This conviction is the deepest and most inspiring influence in theology today; but this conviction is grounded on straightforward historical study of the character of Christ, not on metaphysical speculation. It can be no service to the church, it would seem, under this fresh and independent conviction to react toward a really metaphysical tritheism, affirming social relations and love within the Godhead, in the immanent trinity. The attempt has been widely approved, but I cannot doubt that, so far as it becomes a living faith, it means tritheism pure and simple, and will surely bring its own punishment. This, at least, is true: nothing calls for more absolute and complete personality than love and social relations. To affirm social relations, therefore, in the Godhead is to assert absolute tritheism. And no possible manipulation of the terms can avoid it. The analysis of self-consciousness, also, taken from Hegel—to put it flatly—helps not at all to a real trinity and proves nothing. It is far better that we should admit that we simply do not understand the eternal trinity than that by explanations that do not explain we should be driven to ascribe three persons to God in the only sense in which we can

322

---

[16] The Gospel for an Age of Doubt, p. 110.

understand person, and not be able to say that God is one person in any sense we can understand. This new tritheism seems to me far less defensible than even the oldest credal statements of the trinity, for those were at least scrupulously careful to insist that the distinctions in the Godhead were not personal, but that God was in truth one. We are likely to find the biblical doctrine of the trinity more satisfying both intellectually and religiously than any later abstractly wrought out statements. We believe in one God, our Father, concretely and supremely revealed and brought nigh with absolute and abiding assurance in Christ, and making himself known in the hearts of all who will receive him, in the most intimate, constant, and powerful, but not obtrusive, friendship possible to man, giving thus the supreme conditions of both character and happiness.

Moreover, the religious need of the strict unity of God is very great. I want to know that God himself, the infinite source of all, is my Father; that he, not some second being, loves me. And this is the very significance of Christ that God is in him, speaks and works through him. This seems to be Christ's constant testimony, and the one view that includes both sides of John's representation of him. It is the whole meaning of Christ that he reveals God himself, that we may see God's love in his love. Less than this seems still to leave us far from the gospel, as Luther felt, and underestimates the significance of Christ. "He that hath seen me *hath* seen the Father." Unitarianism emphasizes the *humanity* of Christ to preserve the *unity* of God, the true view emphasizes the *divinity* of Christ to preserve the unity.

(5) But it is the greatest glory of this new sense of the historical Christ that, whether we are able adequately or in agreement to phrase his relation to us or to God, the fact stands out with increasing clearness for all men that simply coming into his presence we find the key to the meaning of life, we find ourselves, we find God. Not apologetically, therefore, not with misgiving, but in glad confidence, we own him Lord. In our intellectual formulations of his person we may not satisfy one another. But "no man can say Jesus is Lord, but in the Holy Spirit." It is hardly possible to mistake, *e.g.*, the note of personal confession and joy in these words of Adolf Harnack: "When God and everything that is sacred threatens to disappear in darkness, or our doom is pronounced; when the mighty forces of inexorable nature seem to overwhelm us, and the bounds of good and evil to dissolve; when, weak and weary, we despair of finding God at all in this dismal world—it is then that the personality of Christ may save us."[17]

When theology tries now honestly to take account of these great convictions of our own age, it only attempts more adequately to conceive the great abiding truths of Christianity, and make them real to *this* generation. It seeks to be more *Christian*—closer to the very spirit and teaching of Christ,

323

---

[17] *Christianity and History*, p. 47.

its supreme authority; more personal and reverent of personality—insisting on the whole man and the personal relations which are essential in every moral and spiritual problem; more *biblical*—with unfaltering faith in the historical revelation of God, and owning the priceless value of the reflections of Christ in his own generation, it means to give a weight to biblical statements in theology that has not yet been given; more *historical*—for it wishes humbly to know the actual way that God has taken, not its own imaginings; more *practical*—for it looks only to life, the highest life; more *ethical*—for it knows that to be a child of God is to be of like character with God; more *social*—for it remembers the great commandment:—Christian, personal, biblical, historical, practical, ethical, social, and, once again and supremely, Christian. "Other foundation can no man lay than that which is laid, which is Jesus Christ." "And this is life eternal that they should *know* thee, the only true God, and him whom thou didst send, even Jesus Christ."